Excruciatingly

GROSS JOKES

W9-CJT-905

ZEBRA BOOKS
KENSINGTON PUBLISHING CORP.

ZEBRA BOOKS

are published by

Kensington Publishing Corp.
475 Park Avenue South
New York, NY 10016

Second printing: April, 1992

Printed in the United States of America

To Debra Dobkin,
a beautiful person
who makes beautiful music.

CONTENTS

Chapter One

GROSS RACIAL AND ETHNIC JOKES

Did you hear about the new Mexican sports car?

It's got four on the floor—and 12 in the back seat.

Did you hear about the new all-black version of "Shogun"?

It's called "Shonuff."

The Polack walked into the bar one night with a big grin on his face and ordered a round of drinks for the house. A buddy asked, "Why are you so happy?"

"Well, last night I got home early, walked into the bedroom, and found my wife in the sack with three guys."

The guy said, "How in the hell could that make you happy?"

The Polack said, "When I asked her what she was doing, she said, 'I told you no one man could take your place.'"

Why did the Polack stick his prick in boiling water?

His wife told him to get sterilized.

Did you hear about the Irishman who decided to write a drinking song?

He could never get past the first few bars.

The guy walked into a bar and saw the Italian guy downing double whiskeys one after another. He walked up and said, "What's wrong?"

The Italian guy shook his head sadly and replied, "I got a problem with my mother-in-law."

"Cheer up. Everybody has trouble with his mother-in-law."

The Italian guy said, "Yeah, but not everybody gets her pregnant."

Did you hear about the Polish inventor who crossed a toaster and an electric blanket?

It was for people who wanted to pop out of bed.

How can you tell if an Italian guy's in the Mafia?

His favorite food is broken leg of lamb.

One JAP ran into another at Bloomingdale's and said, "You look awful, darling. What's wrong?"

The second JAP replied tearfully, "My husband is threatening to leave me."

The first JAP shrugged. "So what's the problem? I tell

my Myron all the time I don't care if he leaves me."
  "You don't?"
  "Not as long as he leaves me enough."

––––––––––––––––

Why wouldn't the Polack buy Christmas seals?

He didn't know what to feed them.

––––––––––––––––

How can you tell if a kid is Scottish?

He's the one who asks for a doggie bag in the school cafeteria.

––––––––––––––––

How can you tell a WASP house?

Their *TV Guide* is in hardcover.

Did you hear about the Puerto Rican burglar?

He was so successful, he stopped making house calls.

———————————

What's the difference between an Italian wife and a JAP wife?

An Italian wife can really cook; a JAP can really dish it out.

———————————

How can you tell if a WASP is a really talented lover?

Last time he made love to his wife, she lost her place in her book twice.

———————————

Did you hear about the Polack who was born at home?

When his mother saw him, she went to the hospital.

The Polish guy walked into his bathroom and saw his wife sitting on the floor, naked, staring at her cunt. He asked, "Is anything wrong?"

"Nah," she replied. "I'm studying for my Pap test."

Who always drives the hottest cars?

Puerto Ricans—everything they drive is stolen.

What's the difference between a young French girl and a young Polish girl?

A young French girl turns heads; a young Polish girl turns stomachs.

How can you tell if a guy is Polish?

Every time he walks into an elevator, the operator says, "Basement?"

What card do all Jewish mothers carry in their wallets?

"In case of an accident, I'm not surprised."

———————————

Did you hear about the new Jewish mothers' softball team?

Every time a player steals second, she feels so guilty she goes back.

———————————

How dumb are Polacks?

Even their wisdom teeth are retarded.

———————————

A Jewish guy was talking to a friend at the temple. He said, "My wife is the most frigid woman in the world. She only lets me screw her once a month, and only if I come home with an expensive present."

His friend grunted. "You think you've got it bad? My wife is even more frigid."

"How do you know?"

"Last week we bought a water bed. Her side froze."

A woman walked up to a Jewish garment company owner at the country club and said, "Mr. Stein, I hate to bother you. But I represent the Save the Children Federation. We want everyone to know that just $25 will support a child in India for an entire year. Will you think about that?"

"I certainly will," Stein replied. Two days later, he shipped his children to India.

The chief of staff came into the Oval Office and told President Bush, "I have some good news and some bad news."

Bush said, "Give me the bad news first."

"A bus full of Japanese tourists has been hijacked in New York."

"What's the good news?"

"We have two million snapshots of the terrorists."

Why don't Jews drink?

It interferes with their suffering.

A Polish girl walked into the doctor's office and said, "I've made up my mind. I want a sex change operation."

The doctor looked at her and asked, "From what?"

Did you hear about the Polack who went on "The Dating Game"?

He chose himself—and scored.

What's the difference between an Irishman and a Moslem?

An Irishman gets stoned before he sleeps with someone else's wife.

The Polack walked into a neighborhood bar and a neighbor called, "Hey, Karlinski, you idiot. You gotta pull down the shades when you're humping your old lady—I could see everything."

Karlinski got a big grin on his face. "You're wrong, Kearney. The joke's on you. I wasn't even home last night."

A Polack sat down at the bar next to this very hot-looking chick. To his amazement, she started coming on to him. A few drinks later, she invited him back to her apartment. She escorted him into the bedroom. He took a look, then exclaimed, "Wow, a water bed."

She smiled, then said, "I'm going to slip into something comfortable."

He waited impatiently, then grinned as she came back into the bedroom stark naked and reclined on the water bed. Unable to restrain himself, the Polack was soon all over her. Things began to get hot and heavy when the girl said, "Before we go any farther, don't you think you should put on some protection?"

"You're right," the Polack said. He left the room, and a few minutes later he came back in wearing a life jacket.

———————————

Why did the Polish wife put a car battery on her husband's side of the bed?

Because she could never get him started.

———————————

What's the perfect gift for a JAP who returns everything?

A boomerang.

Why did the sign outside the Polack swimming club read "Ool?"

They didn't want P in it.

_____

How do Jews protect their bagels?

They put lox on them.

_____

How do you know when a black kid's been crying?

His face is clean.

_____

What's an Italian three-piece combo?

An organ, a cup, and a monkey.

The two Jewish businessmen were playing golf when one said, "It's great to get away from the house. All my wife ever does is ask for money. Why this week alone, she asked for $100 on Wednesday, $150 on Friday, and $75 this morning."

The second Jew said, "That's annoying. Tell me, what does she do with the money?"

The first Jew shrugged. "How would I know? I've never given her any."

———————

Three Jewish businessmen were sitting in a deli in the garment district talking. One said, "Our poor friend Abe Stein, he's in such trouble. He asked me to help him out by taking on his fall line, but it's so ugly I had to say no. Business is business."

The second businessman said, "I know what you mean. My Rebecca was engaged to his Jacob, and Abe pleaded with me to let the marriage go on. But with his prospects, I had to make her call it off. Business is business."

The third businessman said, "Well, I want you to know that Abe came to me, too, and I put him back on his feet."

"You did?" the other two said with surprise. "How did you do that?"

"I repossessed his car."

An elderly Scotsman carrying a huge suitcase boarded a train. A few minutes later, the conductor came around and asked him where he was going.

"Glasgow," the Scotsman grumbled.

"That will be 20 pounds," the conductor said.

"Twenty pounds!" the Scot roared. "Why that's robbery. I never pay more than ten."

"Well, the fare is 20 now, so pay up."

"I'll pay ten and not a shilling more."

"Twenty," the conductor demanded.

"Ten."

"Twenty."

"Ten."

The conductor was furious now. He noticed that the train was passing over a wide river at the time, so he pointed at the valise and threatened, "If you don't give me twenty pounds right now, I'll throw this bag into the river."

The Scotsman's face turned bright red. "I should have known. You're not only trying to rob me, but now you want to drown my poor innocent grandson."

————————

A guy was walking down the street when he saw a Polack frantically searching for something. He went up to him and asked, "Stash, what's the problem?"

"I lost my wallet."

"Ah. So you're looking for your wallet?"

"No," the Polack said. "My brother found my wallet."

The guy was puzzled. "Why that's terrific. But what

are you looking for now?"

"My brother," the Polack replied.

Why did the Polack beat his son after he saw his report card?

He wanted to make him smart.

One Polish girl was instructing another in the art of fellatio. The student said, "I wonder how long dicks should be sucked?"

The first Polish girl said, "The same as the short ones."

What's the most common decoration awarded in the Italian army?

The Yellow Heart.

A black man's car broke down on a rural Mississippi highway, and he decided to head for the next town on foot to get some help. He was about five miles down the road when a redneck carrying a rifle popped out from the brush and said, "Hey, coon, y'all get your hands in the air."

The black man did as he was told. The redneck came up and said, "Now, you stand still while I take your money." He reached into a pocket and got a huge, gap-toothed grin on his face when he found nearly $200 in wadded-up bills.

The black man pleaded, "Mister, I's carrying that money from the congregation to the preacher. They's gonna kill me."

The redneck said, "Tell'um you was robbed."

The black man thought for a moment, then said, "They be suspicious. But I gots an idea." He took off his hat and added, "Would you mind shooting a hole or two through that hat? Then they'll believe me." The redneck obliged.

The black man then took off his coat, asking, "And a couple shots through that?" The redneck shot it three times.

"And how about my vest?"

The redneck said, "Ain't got no more bullets." Immediately, the black man jumped him, wrestled away the rifle, smashed him over the head, tied him up, took the money back, and headed down the road.

The redneck looked at him, shook his head, and muttered, "Proves it, damn straight—you just can't trust a fucking nigger."

The rural Mississippi politician was up at the state capital lobbying against a proposed civil rights bill. He was sitting with the party leadership, including the black majority leader, when he said, "Beg your pardon, but my good old boys are gonna be mad as hornets if that there bill passes—so mad they'll grab their rifles and shoot themselves a few niggers."

The black politician winced. Then he asked, "And if this bill doesn't pass?"

"Hell," the Klansman said, "they'll be so happy they'll probably get drunk as skunks and go out and shoot a few niggers."

———————

A man was sitting in a bar when he noticed his Polish friend walk in. To his amazement, the Polack was walking stiffly with his elbows bent, arms pressed to his sides, and hands extended, palms facing each other about eight inches apart. The Polack sat on a bar stool and ordered a beer. When it arrived, he asked his friend, "Could you lift that glass to my lips for me?"

"Sure," the friend said. He let the Polack sip, then asked, "What happened to you? Was it an accident?"

The Polack shook his head as the bartender arrived with the tab. The Polack said, "Could you pay for this for me? I'll pay you back next time I see you."

Feeling sorry for him, the friend paid. Then he asked, "Tell me, do you have some sort of disease that makes your arms rigid like that?"

"No."

Exasperated, the friend asked, "Then exactly what's your problem?"

"Problem? I don't have a problem. My wife asked me to buy her a pair of shoes and this is her size."

How can you pick out a Jewish mother's tombstone?

It's the one that reads, "I told you I was sick."

A man walked into temple and saw his friend Jacob looking forlorn. He asked, "And what is wrong with you?"

The Jewish businessman said, "Two months ago, my Aunt Sophie died and left me $25,000."

"I'm sorry for your loss. Is that's what's upsetting you?"

Jacob shook his head. "And last month, my grandfather died and left me $50,000."

"Two deaths in two months. No wonder you're sad."

Jacob said, "That's not what's wrong."

"Then what?"

"This month, nothing!"

An Irishman was staggering down Main Street in the wee hours of the morning when he spotted the big clock on City Hall. A few minutes later, a cop driving by spotted him standing on the sidewalk dropping coins. The cop stopped and said, "Hey, what do you think you're doing dropping coins through the sewer grate?"

"Shewer!" the drunk slurred. "I thought I was weighing myself."

———————

Two Polacks met on the street when one asked, "I heard your brother's dead. What happened?"

The second Polack replied, "It's terrible. Lettuce killed him."

"How could lettuce kill him?"

"Well," the second Polack explained, "he bought some lettuce at the store, and he asked the owner how to keep it fresh. The owner told him, 'Put your head in a plastic bag, tie it tight, and put it in the refrigerator.'"

———————

What's the recipe for authentic Mexican fajitas?

It begins, "Steal two pounds of steak . . ."

Did you hear about the Jewish guy who was addicted to LSD?

"Lox, Salami, and Danish."

Little Rufus had been enrolled in the Harlem elementary school for a couple days when he came home and said, "Ma, teacher say I can't go back to school until I's take a bath. She say I got B.O."

Mama got furious, grabbed her pocketbook and her son, and stormed off to school. She barged into the teacher's office, bellied her 250 pounds up to his desk, and said, "My Rufus ain't no pussy—you're supposed to learn him, not smell him!"

The 13-year-old black girl came in nearly an hour late to school and the teacher said, "Crystal, why are you so late?"

The black girl said, "I be late 'cause my brother needed me."

The teacher said, "Well, couldn't he have done what he had to do by himself?"

"I don't think so," Crystal replied. "He was fucking me."

The suburban couple was very socially conscious. As part of their commitment to help the homeless, they went into a city shelter, found a destitute young black girl, and took her into their home to cook and do the housework in exchange for room, board, and a generous salary. The black girl wasn't a very capable or enthusiastic worker, but the couple patiently put up with her and continued to pay her salary.

One day, after two years, the girl came into the dining room and told the couple, "I wants you to know I's pregnant."

The woman said, "How did that happen?"

The girl just shrugged. "Donno."

After talking about the situation, the couple agreed that they couldn't kick her out into the street. Not only did they not fire her, they adopted the baby to save her embarrassment.

A year later, the girl was pregnant again. Again, the couple adopted the baby.

Six months later, the black girl announced, "I's gonna have another baby."

The wife said, "We're disappointed. But of course we'll adopt this child, too."

The girl said, "I'm also gonna quit."

The couple was shocked. Finally, the husband stammered, "How can you even think of quitting?"

The girl said, "I ain't never agreed to do all the work for no family with three children."

Did you hear about the Irishman who couldn't find his glasses?

He drank from the bottle instead.

———————————

Did you hear about the JAP whose nose job got screwed up?

Every time she sneezes, she blows her hat off.

———————————

Why was the Polack named Seven-and-Three-Eighths Orzechowski?

His mother picked his name out of a hat.

———————————

The JAP whined to her husband, "So why won't you buy me a mink coat? I'm always very, very cold."

Her husband replied, "If you already know the answer, why ask the question?"

29

A construction crew had just started repair work on a building in Harlem when the foreman told the crew it was time for lunch. The men put all their tools in a big box, then the boss came over to lock the box. The foreman stopped him, saying, "Don't bother, boss."

The boss said, "But there's over a thousand bucks worth of tools in here."

The foreman said, "So what? You ever hear of a black stealing something to work with?"

Why shouldn't you feel sorry for Puerto Rican babies that are unwanted?

By the time they're fourteen, they'll be wanted in a dozen states.

The bank executive was preparing for a business trip to France, and he called in his temporary secretary, who happened to be Polish. He took out his wallet, handed her a bill, then said, "Go downstairs and get me $50 worth of francs for my trip to Paris."

Ten minutes later, she walked back in with a hundred hot dogs.

The Scottish judge called the next case, and the solicitor for the government said, "Your Excellency, the state requests that both the defendants be committed to an insane asylum immediately."

"What did they do?" the judge asked sternly.

"Well," the solicitor said. "MacTavish over there was caught walking down the street wildly throwing his money away."

The Scottish judge's face grew red with indignation. "The man's a lunatic. Lock him up for five years." Then he pointed to the second man and asked, "What did he do?"

The solicitor said, "He walked behind MacTavish and picked up all the money."

"What's crazy about that?" the judge asked.

"Then he gave the money back to MacTavish."

"The looney bin for life!" the judge ordered.

––––––––––––

How can a woman tell if she's purchased genuine Italian shoes?

No matter what size she buys, they'll keep pinching her.

What did the Indian fakirs do when they received two new sacks of nails?

Had a pillow fight.

_____

Why are Eskimo women so fat?

They can't stop blubbering.

_____

A couple of Irishmen were fed up with paying a fortune for their numerous pints every month, so they decided to brew their own beer. They borrowed a few books from the library, pored over them, gathered the necessary ingredients, and mixed up their first batch.

The wait until it was ready was excruciating. When they opened the keg, they were so proud they decided to take a pint to the local pub keeper, who they hoped would purchase a quantity of the brew. They handed the pint to the Irishman, who took a sip, swished it around in his mouth, and swallowed.

"Well," one of the brewers said, "what do you think?"

The pub keeper replied, "I think your horse has diabetes."

A woman had to go to the doctor, but didn't have a baby-sitter for her infant son. Finally, she called in the Italian gardener and said, "Gino, this is my baby son, my life's treasure. I've got to go out for a little while and I want you to treat him like treasure, too. Understand?"

"I understand," Gino replied.

The woman left. Then the Italian took the baby out to the garden and buried him.

What's unique about hillbilly hospitals?

The maternity ward has a bridal suite.

Why did the horny Italian guy fly to Honolulu?

He heard that the moment you get off the plane, a beautiful girl gives you a lei.

What's the biggest Christian dilemma?

If Jesus was a Jew, how come he's got a Puerto Rican name?

33

Did you hear about the Irish woman whose doctor told her not to touch anything alcoholic?

She threw her husband out of the house.

———————

How can you tell an Irish yuppie?

He's got whiskey in his Water Pik.

———————

Did you hear about the Polack who promised to prevent potholes?

He brushed his street with Crest.

———————

How can you tell an Irishman in a fancy French restaurant?

He's the one trying to decide what wine goes best with whiskey.

How do you know you've moved into the wrong neighborhood?

You take your kid to school and a guy in a suit says, "I be da principal."

———————————

How did the welfare office know the caller was Polish?

She wanted to know how to cook food stamps.

———————————

The Irish couple had thirteen kids and a host of other troubles, but somehow the wife had managed to keep the family fed, clothed, and intact. On their twenty-fifth wedding anniversary, the couple was given a gala party at the local pub by their friends and relatives. There was much eating, drinking, and rejoicing. Finally, at the end of the party, the Irishman climbed up on a table and shouted, "We can't end this party without a final tribute to the one true, wonderful, caring person who made my life worth living all of these long 25 years. I love you dearly." As the crowd cheered, he jumped down off the table and embraced the pub keeper.

Why don't JAPs ever cook dinner at home?

No one's invented a steak that fits in the toaster.

A Polack called the computer store and said, "Hey, that new computer you sold me don't work."

The salesman said, "I told you, you need to insert a floppy disk in the slot and close the door."

So the Polack said, "Thanks," and grabbed his wife's nipple.

What did the JAP have stamped on the bottom of her dishes?

"Dry Clean Only."

Three Jewish mothers were sitting around talking when one said, "My daughter, she's the best in the world. Every summer, she takes me to the beach for two weeks. Every winter, she takes me to Florida for two weeks. No daughter could love her mother more."

The second Jewish mother said, "No, my daughter is the best in the world. Every month she takes me to dinner at the fanciest restaurant in town. Every summer, I get a month at the beach and every winter I get a month in Florida. No daughter could love her mother more."

The third Jewish mother said, "You're both wrong. No daughter could love a mother more than my daughter loves me."

The others asked, "So what does she do?"

"Three times a week, she gets into a cab, goes to midtown, takes an elevator to the office of the most famous psychiatrist in the world, and pays him $100 an hour, *just to talk about me!*"

A Polack and his girlfriend double-dated with friends at the amusement park one night. The couples separated for a while. Then the friend was astounded to see the Polack and his girlfriend sitting soaking wet on a bench.

"What happened?" the guy said.

"It's your fault," the Polack said. "You're the one who said to go to the Tunnel of Love. But it was awful—dark, damp, we couldn't see each other, and we got drenched."

"I don't understand," the guy said. "Was there a leak in the boat?"

"What boat?" the Polack replied.

Why is a Harlem drug dealer like Santa Claus?

Nearly every night, he goes for a slay ride.

The representative from the United Fund stopped by to solicit a contribution from Saul Lebowitz, owner of the huge garment company. He was ushered into the man's plush office, where he made his request.

Saul leaned back, took a puff on his Cuban cigar, and said, "Let me tell you a few things. I have an aging mother with arthritis so bad she can't walk, living in a squalid tenement in Brooklyn. My sister Bessie has ten kids, an unemployed husband, and can feed her family only half the time. My oldest daughter hasn't been the same since she was raped at school and she desperately needs psychiatric help."

The United Fund solicitor said, "That's awful."

"Yeah," Lebowitz said. "And if they haven't been able to get a dime out of me, you haven't got a prayer."

What should you do if you see a Polack walk into a restaurant with a beautiful woman on his arm?

Ask him where he got the tattoo.

Did you hear about the six Irishmen who went on a hunting trip?

In just three days, they killed 21 bottles of whiskey.

An Irishman's beloved wife died, and friends and relatives came from miles around for the traditional lively Irish wake. The next morning, the Irishman was finally awakened by his daughter, who said, "Come on, Da, it's time for Ma's funeral."

The Irishman shook some cobwebs from his brain, then said, "Run along and tell Father O'Reilly we'll not be having a funeral today. Last night was so much fun I figure we'll keep your Ma on ice a couple more days."

The JAP said to her blind date, "A lot of men are going to be miserable when I marry."

"Really," the guy said. "How many men are you going to marry?"

How do black kids learn to put on their underwear?

"Yellow in front, brown behind."

———————————

What's the difference between a Jew and a canoe?

A canoe tips.

———————————

What do Puerto Ricans exchange instead of wedding rings?

Flea collars.

———————————

How can you tell an Italian guy is homesick for his wife?

He's in the kitchen fucking a Brillo pad.

What's the first thing a white girl does when she thinks she's in labor?

Finds out how far it is to the nearest hospital.

What's the first thing a black girl does when she thinks she's in labor?

Finds out how far it is to the nearest dumpster.

———————————

How do black mothers get their kids to stop biting their nails?

They make them wear shoes.

———————————

Why did the Polack wrap part of his Walkman around his cock?

He's heard them called headphones.

What do you know happened when you see an oil slick?

Either an Exxon tanker crashed or four Italians went swimming.

Why did the Polack smash a box of Corn Flakes with a hammer?

He wanted to be a cereal killer.

Why did Allah give Arabs arms?

So their fingers wouldn't smell like their armpits.

What's the difference between a white Boy Scout and a black Boy Scout?

Both will help an old lady cross the street; the black Boy Scout leaves her in the middle.

How do they make Polish sausage?

From retarded pigs.

———————

Did you hear about the Italian organ grinder whose monkey died?

He got 98 applications for replacements—97 blacks and a monkey.

———————

Why did the Polack put ten canaries behind the curtain?

He wanted to open a peep show.

———————

What's a Polish burglar alarm?

Teach the kids how to bark.

What do you call a Mexican in an earthquake?

A jumping bean.

———————————

What do you get when you goose a Mexican ghost?

A handful of sheet.

———————————

What do you call a Mexican with herpes?

Manny Sores.

———————————

What do you get when you cross a black and an Indian?

A Sioux named Boy.

Why did the Polack cut his nose apart?

To see how it ran.

―――――――――

How do you play Mexican music?

Eat a couple bean enchiladas.

―――――――――

What do you call a Mexican with a vasectomy?

A dry Martinez.

―――――――――

What do Polish men do when their wives get their periods?

Give them a sock in the puss.

How do you execute a Mexican?

Sit him in wet cement, let it harden, and wait until he explodes.

———————————

Why do Mexicans eat refried beans?

To get a second wind.

———————————

What's the Super Bowl to a Polack?

One that doesn't back up.

———————————

A Polack was sitting in a bar when he said to a friend, "You know, my wife's a saint. Always doing something to help somebody."

"Like what?"

"Like the homeless problem."

The friend asked, "How does she help the homeless?"

The Polack replied, "When I got home the other night, I found out she gave her nightgown to the poor and let these two guys live in our closet."

Who are the most temperamental people in the world?

The Lebanese—you never know when someone's going to blow up.

Why did the Polack throw away his toilet brush?

He went back to using paper.

What did the Polack do when his girlfriend told him picking his nose was disgusting?

He picked it himself.

Chapter Two

GROSS CELEBRITY JOKES

Why is a tampon like Madonna?

They're both stuck up cunts.

_____

What are Jesse Jackson's chances of becoming president?

Excellent—if the Republicans nominate Yassir Arafat.

_____

How does Joan Collins keep her youth?

She locks him in the closet during the day.

Why is the post office raising the price of stamps again?

They need the money to buy more This Window is Closed signs.

Why isn't Washington mayor Marion Barry running for reelection?

With his record, he's better suited for Congress.

Exactly how much of New York City have the Japanese bought?

Well, when you land at LaGuardia Airport, you have to take your shoes off.

What kind of illumination did Noah have on the ark?

Floodlights.

Why did Russian president Gorbachev cruise 42nd Street when he visited New York?

He was engaging in piece negotiations.

———————————

What would happen if you merged Domino's Pizza with the U.S. Postal Service?

Your pizzas would arrive in 30 hours.

———————————

What's the difference between the sex life of the average American man and the sex life of the average congressman?

The average American man has had seven sex partners since the age of 18; the average congressman has had seven sex partners under the age of 18.

———————————

What kind of punishment did the government have in mind for Imelda Marcos?

Living in a cell for ten years with Manuel Noriega.

Remember all that broccoli sent to George Bush after he admitted he hated the vegetable?

Last week Dan Quayle announced that he hated money.

What's the difference between Roseanne Barr and poultry?

Most poultry is dressed better.

What's a "savings and loan" watch?

The little hand is on the 12 and the big hand is in the till.

Why is Congress so tough on criminals?

When it comes to stealing, they don't like competition.

Why hasn't Dolly Parton ever been the *Playboy* centerfold?

Because you'd never be able to close the magazine.

What's the only thing that's less exciting than hearing Dan Quayle speak?

Watching Roseanne Barr get undressed.

Did you hear that Joan Collins was raped once?

She didn't know it until the check bounced.

If the band plays "Hail to the Chief" when the president enters a room, what do they play when a congressman comes in?

"Send in the Clowns."

Did you hear that Zsa Zsa Gabor got a sore throat?

Before she let the doctor paint her throat, she insisted on calling in a decorator.

———————————

Exactly how fat is Roseanne Barr?

On her charm bracelet hang used license plates.

———————————

Did you hear about the nitwitted Siamese twins?

Everything went in one's ear and out the other's.

———————————

Why did Adam and Eve argue?

She was always putting his pants in the salad.

Why does Dan Quayle travel so much?

Last time he spent a day in his office, he was arrested for loitering.

What was the difference between Election Day and Thanksgiving Day?

On Thanksgiving, we got a turkey for the day; on Election Day, we got a turkey for four years.

Did you hear that President Bush found a way to slow down inflation?

He turned it over to the Post Office.

Why is Dan Quayle such a popular speaker at Republican dinners?

They can charge $100 to get in—and $200 to get out.

Did you hear about the guy who took early retirement from the Three Mile Island nuclear power plant?

He went to Maine and got a job as a lighthouse.

Why is the Hubble Space Telescope like ten martinis?

They both make the night sky fuzzy.

How can you tell if a nuclear power plant is becoming dangerous?

The billing department moves out.

The struggling actor was turned down for part after part, and he'd nearly given up. Then one day an agent called and said, "I get the word that they're casting a play about President Kennedy. I remembered that you resemble him quite a bit."

The actor said, "People have told me that. I'd do anything for a part right now."

The agent said, "With your lack of credits, there's only one way you can succeed. I want you to throw yourself into the role. Read every book ever written about Kennedy. Go through all the newspapers from his presidency. Watch every videotape of him you can find. Then talk like him, dress like him, act like him every minute."

The actor followed that advice, slaving away 24 hours a day until he almost believed he was John F. Kennedy. Finally, the day of the audition came, and the actor was so caught up in the arrogance of being Kennedy that he was brilliant. To his great joy, he got the part.

On the way home, he was assassinated.

———————

Why was Bambi's asshole bleeding?

He'd just made ten bucks.

———————

How did Joan Crawford toilet train her kids?

She wired 220 volts to their diapers.

Who was Tinkerbell's abortionist?

Captain Hook.

How did Captain Hook die?

He wiped with the wrong hand.

What's worse than Roseanne Barr with a stomach ache?

Captain Hook with jock itch.

What's a female private eye?

A Dickless Tracy.

Why is Warren Beatty like Joseph of Nazareth?

They both fucked a Madonna.

_____

How does Madonna remember how big Warren Beatty's penis was?

She took a dick tracing.

_____

Did you hear that Washington, D.C., presented Mayor Barry with an award?

They gave him the kilos to the city.

_____

Why did Dan Quayle refuse when President Bush asked him to go on a round-the-world trip?

He said he'd have no way of getting back.

How did the Feds become suspicious of Mayor Barry?

They found him trying to snort the White House.

Did you hear that the Republicans came up with another clever way to recycle?

They're making all bird cages 8½ × 11 inches so Dan Quayle's speeches won't go to waste.

Who was the first bookkeeper?

Adam. He turned over a leaf and made an entry.

Chapter Three

GROSS ANIMAL JOKES

What's a mutton button?

A sheep's clitoris.

How can you tell a guy is a real pervert?

When he sees an elephant, he exclaims, "Wow, look at that perfect 436-224-436."

A man walked into a psychiatrist's office and said, "Doc, I've got a problem. My wife believes that she's a horse."

"Exactly how does this belief manifest itself?" the shrink asked.

"Well," the man said, "she spends all day and all night naked on all fours."

"My goodness," the psychiatrist exclaimed. "That must be embarrassing."

"I'm used to it by now," the man said. "But that's not the real reason I came."

"I know," the shrink said, "you're concerned that she's eating oats and hay."

"No," the husband said. "They're a lot cheaper than steaks and chops."

"I see. But her . . . her bathroom habits must embarrass you."

"No. We use the manure in the garden."

"Then what is it that bothers you?" the shrink demanded.

"There's three guys who think they're stallions who hang around every day mounting her. Now she's in foal."

———————————

The young chick was racing recklessly around the farmyard. Finally his mother, the hen, came up and said, "Junior, I'm ashamed of you. If your father could see you, he'd turn over in his gravy."

Did you hear about the nearsighted whale that followed the submarine?

Every time it shot off a torpedo, the whale passed out cigars.

Did you hear about the gay whale?

He'd bite off the end of a submarine and eat the seamen.

What did the rich sheep rancher do with the expensive diamond necklace?

Hung it around his girlfriend's neck and said, "This is just for ewe."

Why did the female robin build a nest with a hole in the middle?

She loved laying eggs but hated kids.

A woman ran into an old friend. After a few minutes, the friend said, "I notice you're not wearing a wedding ring, although I heard you got married. What happened?"

The woman turned slightly red and said, "I just got divorced, but I'd rather not talk about it."

The friend prodded: "Come on. I told you all the sordid details about my divorce."

"It's too embarrassing."

"Come on. You have to tell someone."

"Well," the woman said, "what it all came down to was that I caught him fooling around with a female patient."

The friend said, "What's so embarrassing about that?"

The woman replied, "He's a veterinarian."

Did you hear about the farmer who was into S&M?

He always chained up his sheep before he fucked them.

The aging mother was on her deathbed, and one of her last wishes was to find out what was happening with her youngest son, Charlie, a weird sick child who'd run away from home at 16. One of her daughters agreed to track Charlie down, and the old woman clung to life. Finally, the daughter returned and told her mother, "I found

Charlie. And I've got some good news about him and some bad news."

The mother whispered, "What's the good news?"

"He's off drugs, and he spends all of his time stuffing animals."

"And what's the bad news?"

"He's not a taxidermist."

————————

Did you hear about the perverted bird-watcher?

He was always going off on a lark.

————————

Why did the little kid put a monkey in a blender?

He loved Rhesus pieces.

————————

Did you hear about the farmer who fell in love with his cow?

It was udder madness.

What do you give an elephant with diarrhea?

Lots of room.

Chapter Four

GROSS HOMOSEXUAL JOKES

A girl came into the office one morning with a sour expression on her face and a friend asked, "What happened on your date last night?"

"Don't ask."

The friend said, "I thought that guy promised he'd treat you royally."

The girl grimaced. "Well, he arrived with champagne, caviar, and flowers, had a limo waiting outside, then took me to the fanciest restaurant in town. I felt like a princess."

"What's wrong with that?"

"Nothing. Then we went back to my apartment, and I discovered he was a queen."

Two doctors were talking about a colleague. One said, "I hate to talk behind his back, but George really hates homosexuals."

"How can you tell?"

"Well, I was on call with him the other night when this real queen phones in and says he accidentally swallowed a half a bottle of sleeping pills."

"And George wouldn't talk to him?"

The first doctor said, "Oh, George talked to him. He told the fag to have a few drinks and get some rest."

A fag went to the doctor with hemorrhoids, and the doctor prescribed some suppositories. He told the fag, "Make sure you get them in properly. To do that, stand with your ass toward the mirror, then bend over, look through your legs, and insert one."

The fag went home, took off his clothes, and stood by the mirror. But when he bent over and took a look through his legs, he got a tremendous hard-on. He looked at his cock, then said, "Relax, silly. It's only me."

Did you hear about the new AIDS hospital outside of Atlanta?

It's called Sick Fags over Georgia.

What do you get when you cross a homosexual with an insect?

An asshopper.

Why are fags like killer bees?

Their leaders are queens and their pricks are fatal.

Did you hear about the new lesbian-run Baskin-Robbins?

The flavor of the month is anchovy.

Did you hear about the new lesbian-run Baskin-Robbins?

The ice cream cones have hair on them.

How can you tell you're in a lesbian-run Baskin-Robbins?

They hand you the cone upside down.

What's the cone made from?

Dil-dough.

_____

Did you hear they finally jailed all the transvestite hookers?

They charged them with violating the Truth in Lending Act.

_____

Why are fags so polite?

They'll give their seat to anyone.

_____

What's a bisexual gentleman?

A guy who takes out a girl three times before he fucks her brother.

What does a housewife do when she's depressed?

Goes to the department store and tries on a few new things.

What does a faggot do when he's depressed?

Goes to a gay bar and tries a few new things.

_____

A fag was standing at the bar talking to his friend Bruce when another queen swished up to him and interrupted, saying, "Darling, I would love to fuck you."

The fag turned and said, "Butt out."

_____

What does a fag call a wad of cum in a baggie?

Fast food.

_____

Did you read the new book about how AIDS spreads?

It's called *Grim Fairy Tails*.

How did the hairdresser get a bad case of diarrhea?

All he ate were fruits.

A faggot was arrested for sodomy and called his lawyer. After a few hours, the lawyer came up to his cell and said, "You're getting out. I got your sentence reduced to a traffic offense."

"A traffic offense?"

"Yeah," the lawyer said. "You'll plead guilty to tailgating."

How do you know your kid's going to grow up to be a faggot?

When you take him to the zoo, he spends five hours at the grizzly cage watching the bear behinds.

How can you tell you're in Greenwich Village?

The street signs say "Kneel . . . Don't Kneel."

A desperate fag hadn't had sex in days when he finally found a wino who agreed to get blown for $20. But before the wino dropped his pants, he said, "I warn you, I got crabs."

"That's okay," the fag said. "I love seafood."

What's a lesbian's favorite pet?

A lap dog.

What do you call a black fag?

A brotherfucker.

What do Good Humor trucks sell in San Francisco?

Spermsicles.

Why do gay golfers love Mexico?

Every day they have a hole in Juan.

_____

How can you tell if two truckers are gay?

They exchange loads.

_____

Why did the fag beat off into the strawberry preserves?

He wanted a penis butter and jelly sandwich.

_____

What's the new lesbian bumper sticker?

Save a Tree. Eat a Beaver.

Why is a frog like a faggot?

The minute they see a fly, their tongues come out.

———————————

Why do gays love movie ushers?

They can always find a seat in the dark.

Chapter Five

A GROSS VARIETY

The nuns went out to see a movie, then decided to stop for an ice cream sundae. By the time they got back, the gates of the convent had been locked. After some searching, they found a short piece of lumber that they used as a shovel to dig a shallow hole under the fence. As one nun wriggled under, she hissed, "All this digging and crawling stuff makes me feel like a marine."

"Me, too," the other nun agreed. "But their curfew's an hour earlier than ours."

An old codger was sitting on a park bench when he said to his crony, "Gosh darn it, those women have all the luck when it comes to getting old."

"What do you mean?"

"Well," the senior citizen replied, "I can barely remember the last time I was able to get it up in bed. But my wife, she's healthier than ever."

"How is she healthier?"

"Years ago she used to have these terrible headaches near every night before bed. Now, she hasn't had a headache in years."

Why did the Siamese twins move to England?

So the other one could drive.

Why isn't it so bad to be a kleptomaniac?

You can always take something for it.

How did the teenager know he had bad acne?

His dog called him Spot.

_____

How do you know you're really old?

You can remember when there were championship fights between two white guys.

_____

How does a kid know his parents hate him?

He sets the house on fire, and they send him to his room.

_____

Why did the vampire always drive on I-95?

It was the main artery.

The father came home with a brand-new Honda, and after some persuasion agreed to take little Tommy for a spin while the mother cooked dinner. Before they went, the mother said to her husband, "Ted, Tommy's very interested in cars. He'd love it if you pointed out interesting cars while you're driving."

The father and son went out, then returned in a half an hour. The mother asked, "Tommy, did Daddy tell you the names of the cars you saw?"

"He sure did," the boy replied enthusiastically. "We saw two Jaguars, a Ferrari, three Cadillacs, a Corvette, two Lincolns, and 42 Stupid Cocksuckers."

――――――――――

A kid was walking down the street when he spotted his Polish friend. "Hey, Stash," the kid said, "wanna go to the circus with me?"

"Nah," the Polack said. "I'm going to the deli."

The kid said, "You sure? The circus has man eating lions and man eating tigers."

The Polack scoffed, "That's nothing. The deli has a man eating salami."

A gang of hoodlums began hanging out on the steps of the church and hassling worshipers as they came in and out. Finally, the situation got so bad that complaints reached Father Murphy, who decided to go out and talk to the teenagers.

The priest's appearance was greeted by hoots and catcalls. But he went up to the leader and said, "Boys, I think there are better places for you to hang out than on God's doorstep."

The gang leader defiantly said, "Fuck God."

Father Murphy winced. "You're risking God's wrath by breaking His holy laws and taking His name in vain."

The gang leader said, "Fuck God's laws. You name one, I break it. I swear, I fuck, I steal, I smoke, I shoot people. I'll tell you what. I'm gonna break every single fucking law the church has ever made."

The priest said, "Do you really mean that?"

The gang leader turned to his buddies and said, "Do I ever go back on a promise? Blood oath. I'm gonna break every church law."

"Well," the priest said, "I know of at least one sin you haven't committed."

"Yeah? Tell me what it is and I'll do it."

Father Murphy replied, "There's a strict church law against suicide. So kill yourself."

Did you hear about the new organization called DAM?

It's Mothers Against Dyslexia.

Little five-year-old Martha had developed the habit of sucking her thumb, and it drove her mother to distraction. Finally, her mother warned, "Martha, if you don't stop sucking your thumb, your body will swell up until you burst!"

The warning greatly discouraged the little girl. A few days later, she and her mother were walking downtown when they approached a corner where a hooker was displaying her wares. As they waited for the light to change, the little girl stared at the hooker's huge breasts bulging from her tiny halter top and her well-curved hips and buttocks. When her mother started to cross the street, Martha pulled away, ran over to the hooker, and said, "Lady, I know what you've been sucking."

Did you hear about the perverted elementary school music teacher?

He was arrested for fiddling with his students.

The eight-year-old boy called his friend to ask if he could play, but the friend said, "I'm in big trouble. I can't come out."

"What happened?"

"Well," the eight-year-old said, "every night, my mom yells at me to be quiet because the baby is sleeping like a log. So last night I put the damn baby in the fireplace."

_____

A woman said to a friend, "How did your little Ben like his trip to Niagara Falls?"

The mother said, "Why, when we stepped up to the fence, his little face dropped a mile."

"Because he was surprised?"

"No," the mother said. "Because his sister pushed him over the edge."

_____

Two little girls were sitting in the lunchroom of the Beverly Hills elementary school when one said, "Guess what? Mommy's getting married again and I'll have a new daddy."

The second little girl said, "Who is she marrying?"

"Winston James, the director."

The second little girl smiled and said, "Oh, you'll like him. He was my daddy last year."

What's a Beverly Hills PTA meeting like?

297 parents, 21 kids.

———————

How can you tell a kid is a yuppie?

He's making mud pies in a Cuisinart.

———————

The calculating young thing had married the sick, rich old man for his money, and she took great pride in her ability to boss him around. After a few weeks, his condition grew worse and it became time for him to make a new will. As usual, he turned to her before he saw his lawyer and said, "Darling, how should I settle my estate?"

She patted his hand and cooed, "I think you should leave all your money to your greatest source of comfort in these last days of your life."

He nodded agreement, called for his lawyer, then died a few hours later. When the will was read, his wife discovered he'd left $50 million to his electric blanket.

What's the best thing about working for the Vatican?

There's very few office collections for wedding or baby presents.

_____

How can you tell you're getting old?

You have to marinate your Jell-O.

_____

The little boy was in the backyard chasing the cat around with a dish and shouting, "Drink! Drink! Please drink!"

His mother finally heard the commotion, came out, and stopped him. She grabbed the dish, took a sniff, then demanded, "What in heaven's name do you think you're doing trying to feed beer to the cat?"

"I'm trying to get her drunk," the boy replied.

"And why would you do that?" his mother asked.

"For money," the lad replied. "I heard Daddy telling Mr. Jones that he'd pay $100 for a tight pussy."

The elementary school class was visiting the art museum and little Timmy stopped in front of a large painting called *Spring*, which portrayed a very well-endowed nymph covered only by three judiciously placed leaves. Timmy stared and stared until the teacher, impatient to catch up with the rest of the class, said, "Timmy, what are you waiting for?"

"Fall," he replied.

———

A young woman ran into a friend who had recently married an 80-year-old man. "How's your marriage?" she asked.

The new bride grimaced. "That old fart is the most disgusting creature I ever laid eyes on. His wrinkled old body makes me so nauseated I can't eat."

"So why don't you leave him?"

"I am," the bride said. "As soon as I lose another 12 pounds."

———

The mother superior was talking to the priest one day and said, "My nuns are getting very depressed on these long winter nights. Our vows prohibit watching television, listening to music, or reading secular material. I don't know what to do."

The priest thought for a moment, then said, "Mother,

I suggest that you buy a dog. Taking care of another of God's creatures is certainly within the letter and spirit of your vows, and it will provide entertainment besides."

The mother superior thought that was a wonderful idea, and she went out and bought a German shepherd. Two weeks later, the priest arrived for a visit and asked her, "How do your nuns like their pet?"

The head nun replied, "They love the beast, and I have never seen them happier. However, obtaining the dog has produced some very odd behavior."

"What do you mean?"

"Well," she replied. "Last night, I walked downstairs unexpectedly and found the whole convent douching with Gravy Train."

The two brothers were a year apart in age, and the older, bigger brother took a vicious delight in tormenting the younger. Nearly every night, after the lights in their room were out, the bully beat up his brother until the lad said, "Uncle." Then the older brother taunted him saying, "I'll always be older than you. You'll never catch up." The younger brother was so angry that he had trouble sleeping and always came down to breakfast the next morning sullen and depressed.

One morning, however, his mother was astounded to see the younger brother bounding down the stairs whistling a happy tune. She asked, "Why are you so happy?"

The boy said, "You know how Billy's always bragging

that I'll never be older than him? Well, I finally figured out how I can be older than him a year from now."

"And how is that?" the mother asked with some amusement.

"Easy," the boy said with a grin. "I waited until he was asleep, then I smothered him with the pillow."

———————

The gym teacher walked into the boys' bathroom just in time to see little Tommy leave a stall and head for the door. The teacher said, "Didn't your parents teach you to wash your hands after you have a bowel movement?"

"No," Tommy said. "They taught me not to shit on my hands."

———————

The young seminary student came into confession, knelt, and said, "Father, I have a horrible sin to confess. An hour ago, I gave in to temptation and let the bishop give me a blow job."

"God will forgive you, my son," the confessor said. "And the first part of your penance is to suck on a lemon."

"Why do I have to suck on a lemon?" the puzzled student said.

"To get that shit-eating grin off your face," the confessor snapped.

It was retreat week at the seminary when a shocked priest rushed into the bishop's office and said, "Your Excellency, you must come at once." The cleric led the bishop down a set of winding stairs into the kitchen, where three priests were stacked like pancakes, each butt-fucking the one in front of him.

The outraged priest said to the bishop, "Have you ever seen anything like that? What do you think?"

The bishop shook his head. "Lucky Father Reilly. He always gets to be in the middle."

———————

What did Joseph do when he woke up one Sunday morning and discovered his wife got her period?

He had a bloody Mary before brunch.

———————

What's wrinkled and hangs out your underwear?

Your grandmother.

Why did the retired tree surgeon get kicked out of the nursing home?

He went around trying to prune off dead limbs.

Chapter Six

GROSS MEDICAL JOKES

How does a photographer get a group of doctors to smile?

He says, "Say fees!"

What's wrong with seeing a psychiatrist?

When you start, you're slightly cracked; when you're finished, you're totally broke.

Why are proctologists so gloomy?

They always have the end in sight.

The teenager got into crack in a big way, and he finally had to burglarize a dozen homes a day to support his habit. Inevitably, he was caught. Since he was a first offender, he was sentenced to a year of drug rehabilitation and counseling from a specially trained psychologist, Dr. Reynolds.

The teenager was belligerent at first, but the patient therapist gradually brought him around. At the end of the year, the teenager was getting good grades in school, held a part-time job in a gas station, and spent weekends as a volunteer at a nursing home. At his final session, the teenager said to Dr. Reynolds, "I'm a changed person since we first met. I don't smoke crack, I don't lie. I don't steal. I don't know how I can ever thank you."

"Well," the doctor replied. "If you do start smoking crack again, I could use a new color TV."

———————

Why did the female dentist go to the singles bar every Friday night?

At the end of the week, it was her turn to be drilled.

A woman was sitting in the waiting room for what seemed like an eternity when the doctor finally came out. He said, "Mrs. Higgins, I'm sorry the tests took so long. I was going crazy trying to diagnose your urine test until I finally realized what was in the bottle was apple juice."

The woman shouted, "Oh, my God," and ran for the phone.

"Mrs. Higgins, what's wrong?" the doctor asked.

She replied, "Now I know what's in my daughter's lunch box."

———————————

What happened to the plastic surgeon whose dick was too small?

He decided to hang himself.

———————————

Why do all deaf doctors specialize in gynecology?

They can read lips.

The very beautiful young girl lying on the couch was in tears as she told the psychiatrist, "Dr. Harmon, I don't know how to thank you. Before I came here, I was so depressed I felt like killing myself. Now, I have hope. But to make the experience complete, I'd like you to kiss me."

The red-faced psychiatrist said, "I'm afraid I can't do that. That's strictly a breach of ethics. Why, I shouldn't even be lying here naked on top of you."

––––––––––––––

A very huge but very crazy man wandered away from the mental institution and managed to fall into an icy river. A teenage boy was riding by when he saw the accident. Heroically, the boy tied a rope to a tree, lowered himself into the dangerous waters, and managed to drag the much larger lunatic to shore.

About five minutes later, a number of police cars and ambulances came roaring up. A doctor asked the nut, "Who saved you?"

The guy pointed to a tree.

The shocked doctor said, "You mean that boy saved your life, then took his own?"

"Nah," the crazy said. "He said he was wet, so I hung him up to dry."

A man walked into a shrink's office and said, "Doc, you've got to help me. Every night I have the same dream—I'm stranded on a desert island with a dozen gorgeous nymphomaniacs."

"That's not a problem," the psychiatrist said. "Most people have erotic fantasies."

"Yeah," the guy said. "But there's one more thing—in my dream, I'm a woman."

————————

How do you know you have bad breath?

You walk into the dentist's office and he takes laughing gas.

Chapter Seven

GROSS CANNIBAL JOKES

How would you describe the average cannibal?

A guy who had a wife and ate children.

An explorer was deep in the African jungle when he came across a village. Cautious, he entered with rifle ready and confronted the chief. "I mean no harm," the explorer said. "But I must know the answer to one question. Do you practice cannibalism?"

"Absolutely not," the chief replied.

The explorer put away his weapon and entered the village. Immediately, the chief ordered men to seize him, strip off his clothes, and toss him in a pot of water. As the natives built a fire under the pot, the explorer protested to the chief, "You said you didn't practice cannibalism."

"We don't," the chief said. "We're already very good at it."

What did the cannibal say when he first saw a skating rink?

"What do you know, people on the rocks!"

The missionary, despite the gravest danger of the loss of his own life, managed to convert the cannibal chief to Christianity. One of his first pastoral functions was to inform the chief that it was against the laws of his new religion to have five wives.

The chief asked, "You sure Jesus said I only can have one wife?"

"That's right," the missionary said, pleased that the chief appeared to accept the word of the Lord.

The next day, the chief ate four of his wives.

What happened when the cannibal saw a restaurant advertising "All You Can Eat"?

He had two waiters and a busboy.

Did you hear about the nymphomaniac cannibal?

Every time the tribe ate a missionary, she insisted on the bone.

———————

What happens if you attend a cannibal religious ceremony?

You'll be thoroughly stirred.

———————

The cannibal chief was sent to Washington, D.C., on a diplomatic mission, and he brought his family along. It was the end of December, and the Africans were in awe of the snow, the cold weather, and the very odd customs connected with the holidays. On Christmas, the entire family was invited to the house of a State Department official. As the group stood around, the diplomat asked the little cannibal boy, "Son, did Santa Claus stop at your house last night?"

"Yes," the lad said. "And he was delicious."

Why did the cannibal put a Mexican in the blender?

He wanted bean soup.

_____

Why don't cannibals eat Jewish children?

They're always spoiled.

_____

How can you tell a gay cannibal?

He always blows lunch.

_____

What's a cannibal bachelor party?

A girl jumps out of a cake, then everyone has a piece.

Chapter Eight

GROSS SEX JOKES

Assignment: Give a short speech on sex.

Speech: "It gives me great pleasure. Thank you."

A guy walked into a bar and saw his buddy groaning as he downed a double whiskey. As the guy approached, he noticed his buddy had two black eyes and a big bandage covering his nose. The guy asked, "What happened to you?"

The buddy mumbled, "Seenus."

The guy was puzzled. "Don't you mean 'sinus'?"

The buddy said, "Nah. Last night I was screwing my next-door neighbor and her husband seen us."

What's a doggie bra?

It makes pointers out of setters.

_____

A guy was boarding a crowded elevator when he inadvertently jabbed a young lady in the chest with his elbow. He liked what he felt, so he said to her, "If the rest of you is as terrific as those tits, I'd love to fuck you."

She replied, "If your cock is as hard as your elbow, come to Room 738."

_____

How can you tell your date's a loser?

When you check into your motel room, he puts a Please Disturb sign on the door.

_____

Why do nudists have the best parties?

When you go out on the dance floor, things are really swinging.

How did the hooker know the cop meant business?

When he showed her his nightstick.

_____

Did you hear about the massage parlor girl who rubbed her customers the wrong way?

Instead of coming, they went.

_____

The very well-proportioned young lady arrived for an interview as an executive secretary. The vice-president closed the door of his office, then said, "Miss Jones, before I hire you, I want to conduct one test. I want you to take down everything I say."

"I'm ready when you are," she replied.

"Good. Let's begin: your skirt, your panties . . ."

_____

What's the difference between a hooker and a sperm bank?

In the average day, a hooker gets more deposits.

Two guys were sitting at a bar when a gorgeous redhead sauntered in and sat at a table. One guy nudged the other and asked, "Who is that?"

The second guy replied, "Her name is Janice, but around here we call her Pet Store."

"Why Pet Store?"

"Every night about this time she comes in to sell a little pussy."

———————

How can you tell your date's really ugly?

You take her to dinner, and the waiter puts her food on the floor.

———————

How can you tell if a guy's a loser?

He hires a hooker and she tells him, "Not on the first date."

What's the definition of a faithful Hollywood husband?

One whose alimony checks arrive on time.

———————

Why is a hooker like a Xerox salesman?

They both lease reproduction equipment.

———————

A guy came up to a friend at the bar and asked, "Who was that man you were just talking to?"

"A private detective. I hired him to follow my wife."

"No!" the guy exclaimed. "What's wrong? Is your wife screwing somebody on the side?"

"No," the friend replied. "But I am, and I want to know where she is when I'm doing it."

———————

Did you hear about the congresswoman who changed careers?

Instead of running for reelection, she put her seat up for sale.

A guy walked into a bar and sat down next to a friend. The friend said, "I thought you were out shopping with your wife."

"I was," the guy replied as he ordered a beer and a shot. "But we had a fight."

"What about?"

The guy said, "She was after me to buy a pair of those designer jeans. I told her that if I was gonna pay 80 bucks for a pair of jeans, I expect a good-looking broad to be in them."

———————

How can you tell a woman is really flat?

She applies for a job as a topless waitress and gets hired as a busboy.

———————

A guy was sitting at the bar when a friend said, "Why are you here tonight?"

The guy replied, "My wife threw me out of the house for being honest."

"How's that?"

"Well, we were watching TV when she asked me, 'What can I do to make you more interested in sex?' And I said, 'Leave town.'"

Did you hear about the executive who didn't believe in wasting time on secretaries?

His motto was, "If at first you don't succeed, fire her."

———————————

How can you tell if a guy is a loser?

His only sex life is when a doctor tells him to cough.

———————————

Why are impotent men immature?

They were born, but never raised.

———————————

Why is a whorehouse like a cemetery?

In a whorehouse, you can rest in piece.

Why is a hooker like a cattle rancher?

They both raise meat.

———————

Did you know that all hookers use very poor grammar?

They end every sentence with a proposition.

———————

A husband came home from work one day to find his wife red-faced and furious. He asked, "What's wrong?"

She said, "I was downtown shopping when I saw you go into a hotel with a young blond on your arm. I want an explanation, and I want the truth."

The husband said, "Well, make up your mind—which do you want?"

———————

What's the difference between courtship and marriage?

In courtship, a woman plays hard to get; once you're married, she's impossible to get.

A woman was sitting with her friend at the country club when the friend said, "You know, for the last year or so, I haven't been able to figure out where Reggie was spending his nights."

The friend replied, "Darling, why didn't you hire a private detective?"

"Well, I was just about to," the friend replied. "Then one evening I went home early, and there he was!"

There was a severe shortage of available women in the remote area of Wyoming. After almost a year without companionship, the rancher sent for a catalog from a lonely hearts club, picked out a picture, and started a correspondence. After a few letters, he concluded arrangements for a marriage.

He was all dressed up in his finest when the train arrived. To his delight, the very well stacked blond who exited from the car was even more beautiful than the picture he had fallen in love with. He escorted her to his pickup truck, drove directly to the justice of the peace, had the short ceremony performed, then eagerly sped home for the long-awaited honeymoon.

Shy from being alone, he turned off the light as he waited in bed. When his partner slipped under the covers, he rolled over and began to caress her. Then, he sat up abruptly in shock as his hand felt a huge, throbbing dick. He sat up in bed, flicked on the light, and saw that his "wife" was a transsexual with big tits and a big cock. "What's the meaning of this?" he demanded.

The "she-male" looked at him in surprise. "You mean you didn't know? After all, you sent for a male order bride."

———————

A guy was complaining about his wife when his buddy said, "My wife is even worse. She treats men like dirt."

"How so?"

"Every night I come home early, she makes one hide under the bed."

———————

What's the difference between a BMW and a baby carriage?

A baby carriage is last year's fun on wheels.

———————

The ladies at the club were complaining about panhandlers. One lady said, "I'm ashamed to admit that I gave in and handed over $20 to a bum yesterday."

A second lady said, "I felt so sorry for a poor woman that came to the door that I gave her a whole ham for her family."

A third lady said, "I want you to know that I gave in and screwed a bum last night."

"What did your husband say?" another lady asked.

"He rolled off and said thank you," she replied.

Why did they call the coed "Turnpike"?

Once you got on, you never had to stop.

How can you tell an executive's secretary is a lousy lay?

When he chases her around the desk, he walks.

A guy walked into a bar and saw his friend, who sold helicopters, putting away doubles like there was no tomorrow. The guy asked, "What's wrong?"

The salesman said, "You remember I told you I had this sheik from Saudi Arabia coming over to look at our new line? Well, yesterday, he arrived. I had a 50-foot limo pick him up at the airport, I had all the brass out at the factory to greet him, I got an air force general to take him for a flight in the bird, and I had the fanciest restaurant in town cater a 20-course meal. On top of that, I laid out two grand for the best hookers in town to take care of the sheik back at his penthouse."

"And after all that, the sheik didn't place an order?"

"On the contrary. He ordered 300 more."

"Three hundred more helicopters. That's fantastic!"

"No," the salesman said bitterly. "He ordered 300 more girls."

Did you hear about the whore who got fired by the madam?

She was caught standing up on the job.

A man was driving to work one day when he saw his golfing buddy, a prosperous lawyer, waiting at the bus stop. He pulled over, offered him a lift, then asked, "What's the matter? Your car in the shop?"

The lawyer said, "No. My BMW was stolen last Friday."

"And the cops haven't been able to find it?" the friend asked.

"Actually, I haven't reported it to the police yet. I have mixed feelings about the whole thing."

"How could you have mixed feelings about your BMW being ripped off?"

"Because," the lawyer said, "my wife was in it."

———————

Did you hear about the Wall Street firm that merged with an S&M brothel?

They now offer stocks and bondage.

———————

What's the difference between life in A.D. 990 and life in A.D. 1990?

In A.D.990, men rode chargers; in 1990, they marry them.

———————

A young man walked into his girlfriend's father's study and said, "Mr. Smith, I want to marry your daughter."

The father looked at him sternly, then asked, "Have you seen Mrs. Smith?"

The young man said, "Yes, she's a good enough lay. But I still prefer your daughter."

Miss Primpton, the wealthy and extremely snobbish town spinster, spotted a 22-year-old man at a town meeting and said loudly, "Richard, I'm going to have to tell your mother you've been drinking again. I saw your car parked in front of the tavern last night."

With half the town staring at him, the young man's face turned bright red. About 9:00 p.m., he parked his car outside the spinster's house and left it there all night.

A guy was sitting in a bar when he said to his friend, "How about going to the ball game with me tomorrow night?"

"Sorry," the guy said. "But the symphony is playing Mozart that night."

"What about Saturday night?"

"The symphony is playing Brahms."

"Sunday?"

"The symphony is playing Tchaikovsky."

"Christ," the first guy said. "I didn't know you loved classical music so much."

"I hate classical music," the second guy said. "But whenever the symphony plays, I go over and fuck the conductor's wife."

What's a mistress?

What goes between a mister and a mattress.

———————————

What's a sin of omission?

Any sin you forget to commit.

———————————

How do you know when it's *really* cold in the house?

It cures your wife's headache.

———————————

The two hookers met in the coffee shop and one noticed the other continually scratching her snatch. "What's wrong?" she asked.

The second hooker said, "I got this infection that itches like crazy."

"What are you taking for it?"

"Just about anything a john offers me."

A lawyer walked into his partner's office, closed the door, and said, "Sam, mind if I ask you a personal question?"

"Go ahead."

The lawyer said, "Are you by any chance screwing our new receptionist?"

Sam admitted, "I am. I took her to the Plaza a couple nights ago. I'll tell you, she's a tiger. Compared to her, fucking my wife is like fucking a fire hydrant."

The other lawyer walked out, deep in thought. A couple weeks later, Sam walked into his office, closed the door, and asked, "Mind if I ask you a personal question? Are you fucking our new receptionist now?"

The partner said, "I have to admit I am. And you're right—compared to her, fucking your wife is like fucking a fire hydrant."

———————

A husband had been feuding with his wife, but his anger reached a new height when he stopped by the bank to cash a check and was told the account was empty. He stormed into the house and said, "How dare you take all the money out of our account?"

"It's my turn," she said.

"What do you mean, your turn?"

"Well," she said, "in bed, you've been making early withdrawals for years."

What's the difference between your wife and Jello-O?

Jello-O moves when you eat it.

_____

What happened to the woman who swallowed a razor blade?

In a week, she gave herself a hysterectomy, castrated her husband, circumcised her lover, took two fingers off her girlfriend's hand, and gave her minister a harelip.

_____

How do you know your wife's been talking to your daughter about you?

Your daughter says she wants to be a widow when she grows up.

_____

What do you do for a Peeping Tom who's leaving the neighborhood?

Throw him a bon voyeur party.

117

What do you call a girl who works for a telephone sex service?

A conversation piece.

———————

Why is it painful to fuck a chef?

He'll stick a fork in you to find out if you're done.

———————

Why was the loser so frustrated?

He finally woke up with an erection only to discover both his hands were asleep.

———————

A man came home one night to find his wife lying naked in bed, sobbing. He asked, "What's wrong?"

She said, "A couple hours ago a gigantic black man broke into the house. He made me suck on his prick, which was so huge I nearly choked. Then he turned me over and fucked me in the ass. Finally, he peed on me while I had to sing the national anthem."

The shocked spouse said, "Darling, that's horrible."

"It certainly was," she said. "You know how hard it is to sing the national anthem."

How do you know your date's a loser?

His favorite sex aid is Fix-a-Flat.

What's the difference between a parachute and a prophylactic?

When a parachute fails, somebody dies.

A group of women were complaining about their husbands when one said, "My husband is the absolute worst. All he ever thinks about and dreams about is golf. I can't get him to look at me, let alone touch me."

Another woman said, "My husband's also a golf fanatic. But I found a way to attract his attention."

"What do you do?"

"I wait until he's just about to go to bed. Then I take a flag and stick it in my hole."

The guy had finally got the chick into the sack and things were getting hot and heavy. He started to get inside her when she murmured, "Slow down, baby. Foreplay is an art."

The guy panted, "Well, you better get your canvas arranged soon, babe, or I'm gonna spill my paint."

———————————

What's a vasectomy?

A stitch in time that saves nine.

———————————

How do you know a guy's a loser?

He calls a telephone number on the men's room wall and gets Dial-a-Prayer.

———————————

What's the best way to stop a guy from smoking after sex?

Fill his water bed with gasoline.

Why are anchovies like telephones?

They're the next best thing to being there.

———————————

The ardent women's libber was arguing, "I believe that women are the foundation of our country."

"I agree," the male chauvinist replied.

"You do?" she said with surprise.

"But," the man said, "remember who laid the foundation."

———————————

What can a girl put behind her ears to make her sexy?

Her knees.

———————————

What's the golf tournament for flashers?

The Zipper Open.

121

Why do carpenters make lousy lovers?

They're used to putting their tools in a box after they're done.

———————————

How do you know your date's a loser?

All his soap has holes drilled in it.

———————————

How do you know your date's a loser?

His teddy bear has an artificial vagina.

———————————

How do you know you've got a small penis?

Your date asks you if she can use it to get out a splinter.

How do you know a woman's got a huge cunt?

The only guy who will go to bed with her is a spelunker.

––––––––––––––––––

How do you know who you should fuck today?

Look it up in your whoroscope.

––––––––––––––––––

Why is Kotex such a potent international weapon?

It keeps the Reds in, the Poles out, the Greeks happy, and the French hungry.

––––––––––––––––––

What do you call it when a hooker comes to your hotel room?

Womb service.

How do you celebrate a vasectomy?

With a bottle of Dry Sac.

———————

When should you wear two rubbers?

When it's raining.

———————

A guy went to see a shrink and said, "Doc, I'm worried about my wife."

"What's the problem?"

"Well," the guy said, "yesterday she posed for a nude picture."

The shrink said, "A lot of women like to pose in the nude."

"For a driver's license?"

———————

How can you tell if your wife is ugly?

A mosquito bites her, then throws up.

The guy walked into the bar and said, "I managed to get you a blind date for the wedding."

"What's she like?" his friend asked.

"Well, there's good news and bad news. The good news is she's a model."

"Wow! That's great."

"The bad news is she models for cello cases."

It isn't running around with women that will get you.

It's the pit stops.

Why is it hard to pronounce "fellatio"?

It's a mouthful.

Why is a penis like payday?

It can't come too often.

Chapter Nine

SIMPLY DISGUSTING

What's the best way to prevent forest fires?

Pee on a tree.

———————

What's the definition of a bad day?

Going upstairs to change out of your wedding gown and finding blood on your panties.

———————

Why did the Polack shove his sneaker up his ass?

He wanted to make a tongue-in-cheek remark.

How did the necrophiliac have his way with women?

He'd just show up and knock them dead.

––––––––––––––––

A kindly woman was walking down the street when she saw a heartrending sight. Standing on the sidewalk were a grown man and a three-year-old boy. Each was wearing sunglasses and holding a cup. The little boy was wearing a sign that read, Blind from Birth.

Moved, she placed a generous contribution in each cup. Then she said to the man, "You must have been so heartbroken that your son was born blind."

The man said, "He wasn't born blind, lady. We poked his eyes out."

The horrified woman demanded, "Why would you do such a horrible thing?"

The blind begger said, "We wanted him to get a good start in life."

––––––––––––––––

How long do rednecks cook their meat?

Until the tire marks disappear.

Where does a redneck go for take-out food?

Highway 101.

———————————

A wealthy businessman was chasing a beautiful young secretary in his office, but she steadfastly refused all his advances. Finally, he cornered her in his office late one night and said, "I'll give anything to fuck you. Just name it."

The secretary said, "All right. I'll sleep with you if you make sure I have all the money I need for the rest of my life."

The businessman thought for a moment, then said, "Okay. I agree. I promise you'll have all the money you'll need for the rest of your life. And I'll put it on paper."

He pulled out a pad, wrote down the promise, signed it, and gave it to her. She put it in her purse, took off her clothes, and lay down on the couch.

He fucked her vigorously. When it was over, he said, "That was so good I'll give you more money than you'll ever need for the rest of your life."

"That's great," she said.

So he handed her a $20 bill, then strangled her.

Two Polish guys went hunting and got separated in the woods. Sure enough, one mistook the other for a deer and shot him. It was nearly an hour before the Polack got help to get his friend out of the woods and to a hospital. After the emergency room doctor looked the patient over, the Polack asked anxiously, "Will he make it?"

"I don't know," the doctor replied. "It would have been better if you hadn't gutted him and skinned him."

A man went to the doctor complaining that he was always eating but was still losing weight. The doctor examined him, took X-rays, then said, "I'm afraid you have a tapeworm—a big one. It might take us some time to get him."

The man was given a prescription for one drug, then a second drug, then a third. Nothing worked, and he was getting thinner by the day. Finally, in desperation, he walked into a gypsy fortune-teller's place, told his sad tale, and said, "If you don't see any hope in my future, I think I'll kill myself."

The gypsy said, "Do not fear. For a mere $1,000, I promise your tapeworm will be gone in a week. But you must swear that you'll follow my instructions."

The man swore. The gypsy said, "Go home. Three times a day for six days, you must take a hot dog and shove it all the way up your ass. Then immediately afterward, insert five M&M's. On the seventh day, come back here."

The guy thought it was bizarre, but he did what he was told. On the seventh day, he came back to the fortune-teller, who grabbed a big hammer and escorted him into another room. The gypsy instructed him to drop his pants, sit on the edge of a table, shoot a hot dog up his ass, and wait. A couple minutes later, the tapeworm poked his head out of the guy's asshole and bellowed, "Where's my fucking M&M's—"

Splat!

What's the biggest advantage of being a cannibal abortionist?

You don't have to go out for lunch.

How can you tell a kid is Ethiopian?

His pet's a tapeworm.

What's Ethiopian circumcision?

Butt-fucking your sister and letting the tapeworm take off the tip.

What's printed on a necrophiliac's towels?

His and Hearse.

Did you hear about the necrophiliac who sent anonymous love letters to women?

He signed them all, "Eventually yours."

How can you tell if a pervert is a pedophiliac?

Instead of syphilis, he gets diaper rash.

Did you hear about the yuppie necrophiliac?

He had a coffin that was a water bed.

How can you tell if a hospital patient has AIDS?

They give him his shots with a dart gun.

_____

How do you know you've had an underprivileged childhood?

When you go to camp and discover bread isn't supposed to be green.

_____

How can you tell a gay pedophile?

He's always got his dick in the baby-shitter.

_____

How does a necrophiliac beat the summer heat?

He goes down to the morgue and has a cold one.

A guy came home from work late and in a horrible mood. His wife said, "What happened, George?"

"I got a flat tire from running over a milk bottle. Ruined my whole fucking day."

"Didn't you see the bottle?"

"Nah!" George groused. "The damn baby had it under its blanket!"

The two-year-old boy urgently needed surgery to correct a congenital heart defect, but the family was desperately poor. Finally, a friend told the mother about a new documentary television show that featured live surgery. The mother called the producers and arranged for the nation's leading specialist to perform the operation during prime time.

The mother kissed the frightened toddler as he was anesthetized and wheeled into the operating room. Unfortunately, the televised surgery took a horrible turn for the worse after a few minutes and the child died. Quickly, the host of the show ran in to interview the mother. To his surprise, she was grinning. When she saw the microphone and camera she waved and said, "Hi, Ma. Hi, Sis. Hi, Pop."

The host said, "What about your poor little baby that just died?"

The mother shrugged and said, "That's show biz."

To her horror, the teenage girl discovered she was pregnant. Unable to tell her parents, she decided her only course was to end it all. She found a rope, went out to the garage, climbed up on the hood of the car, swung the rope over the rafter, tied a noose around herself, and jumped.

A moment later her ten-year-old brother walked into the garage, saw his sister writhing from the end of the rope, then continued on into the kitchen. His mother said, "Billy, where's Jane?"

The boy said, "She's in the garage hanging herself from the rafters."

"Oh, no!" the mother screamed. "Did you cut her down?"

"Nah," the boy said. "She wasn't done yet."

———————————

The hospital director walked into the operating room just as the Polish surgeon was sawing off the patient's arm. "How's the operation going?" he asked.

"Operation?" the surgeon asked. "I'm doing an autopsy."

———————————

A man was brought into the psychiatric ward in handcuffs. Shortly afterward, a staff physician came into the man's room and asked, "Why are you here?"

"I was arrested for screwing a three year old in the

ass," the man replied.

"My God!" the shocked shrink exclaimed. "Was it a boy or a girl?"

The man snapped, "A girl, of course. What do you think I am, a pervert?"

Why do women have legs?

So you don't have to drag them into the bathroom to douche after you fuck them.

A man escorted his fiancée into Tiffany's, where an elegantly dressed salesman helped them pick out an engagement ring. They were looking at an exquisite diamond that caught the young lady's fancy when the man suddenly let out a loud fart. His fiancée, embarrassed, quickly apologized for him.

The salesman said, "Madam, it is quite expected. In fact, when he finds out how much that ring costs, he's going to shit."

After a dozen years in prison, the convicted forger was released, and he was determined to go straight. With some effort, he found a job, rented an apartment, and found an older, never-married woman who soon fell in love with him. One Saturday afternoon, they decided to drive to Las Vegas to get married. After the ceremony, they were headed back to their hotel when the ex-con excused himself, ducked into a grocery store, then came out holding a paper bag. When they got into the hotel room, the guy opened the bag and pulled out a cucumber.

His bride smile. "That was thoughtful of you, dear, but now that I have you, I don't need one of those any more."

The ex-con said, "Oh, this isn't for you. Even though I've been out a couple months, I still can't fall asleep without something stuck up my ass."

———————————

Two homeless women met in the subway station one day and one said, "Things are getting real bad. I screwed a guy for ten bucks yesterday just so I could get a flop for the night."

"You think that's bad?" the other said. "I blew a guy for free last night just so I could have something warm in my stomach."

What's the difference between a bag of fertilizer and the cheeks of your ass?

Nothing. You get the same smell spreading either one.

Two guys were talking in the bar when one said, "How you coming with that gorgeous babe who moved in next door?"

The other guy growled, "She teased me and led me on for weeks, then wouldn't deliver. But I got even with her."

"What did you do?"

"I took a hammer and nailed her thighs together."

"You did what?"

The guy shrugged. "If you can't lick 'em, join 'em."

How can you tell a mother's a child abuser?

You see her dipping her baby's rectal thermometer in Ben Gay.

A man walked into a drug store and asked the pharmacist, "Do you have any black rubbers?"

The pharmacist replied, "I don't think so. Why do you need them?"

The man said, "My best friend just died."

The pharmacist said, "And you want to bury him with a black condom?"

"Oh, no," the man said. "I just want to be appropriately dressed when I fuck his widow."

Two women were sitting in an abortion clinic. One very nervous young lady watched an older, calmer lady as she rhythmically worked a pair of knitting needles. Finally, the younger woman said, "I hate to say anything. But isn't it a little sick to be knitting little booties before you have an abortion."

The older lady replied, "Oh, this isn't a bootie. It's a body bag."

How can you tell you're in Ethiopia?

You throw up, and there's 20 people lined up behind you with straws.

How did the mother know her daughter was masturbating during her period?

She caught her red-handed.

What's the best way to stop your husband from smoking in the bathroom?

Pour gasoline in the toilet bowl.

What's an abortion?

Love's labors lost.

Where do cannibals buy their caviar?

Abortion clinics.

Why did the wife pee all over her husband?

She wanted to celebrate a golden anniversary.

———————————

What's gross?

Fucking a woman and her tapeworm gives you head.

———————————

What's green, lies on the side of the road, and stinks?

A dead Girl Scout.

———————————

What do you call a girls' softball team that all have their periods?

The Red Socks.

What did the Polack do when the store was out of orange
Kool-Aid?

Bought cherry and peed in it.

_____

How can you tell you're in Ethiopia?

Little kids follow you around waiting for you to pick
your nose.

_____

The oral surgeon came into the waiting room and told
the husband, "I'm afraid there was a complication in
your wife's operation—we had to amputate her lips."

"Oh, no!" the husband said.

The surgeon continued, "But we got a lucky break.
In the next operating room, a woman with the exact same
blood type as your wife's died from a car accident. Her
face had been destroyed, but we were able to transplant
her cunt lips to your wife."

The husband was skeptical, but when he saw his wife
she looked pretty much the same. Three weeks later, the
surgeon ran into the husband on the street and asked,
"How's your wife doing?"

"Good and bad," the husband replied. "The good thing
is that she has an insatiable appetite for oral sex. The bad

thing is that she insists on wearing a beard and won't eat anything but anchovies."

———————————

The wife sat in the lawyer's office and said, "I want to divorce my husband."

"Why?" the attorney asked.

"He brings his work home with him nearly every night."

"A lot of men do that," the lawyer commented.

"But my husband's a mortician."